What is it like now...?

At the seaside

HEINEMANN
LIBRARY

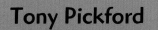

Tony Pickford

www.heinemann.co.uk/library
Visit our website to find out more information about Heinemann Library books.

To order:
☎ Phone 44 (0) 1865 888066
🖹 Send a fax to 44 (0) 1865 314091
💻 Visit the Heinemann Bookshop at www.heinemann.co.uk/library to browse our catalogue and order online.

First published in Great Britain by Heinemann Library, Halley Court, Jordan Hill, Oxford OX2 8EJ, a division of Reed Educational and Professional Publishing Ltd. Heinemann is a registered trademark of Reed Educational & Professional Publishing Ltd.

OXFORD MELBOURNE AUCKLAND JOHANNESBURG BLANTYRE
GABORONE IBADAN PORTSMOUTH (NH) USA CHICAGO

Designed by Celia Floyd
Illustrations by Jo Brooker
Originated by Dot Gradations
Printed in Hong Kong/China

ISBN 0 431 15003 6   (hardback)   ISBN 0 431 15009 5   (paperback)
07 06 05 04 03   07 06 05 04 03
10 9 8 7 6 5 4 3 2 1   10 9 8 7 6 5 4 3 2 1

British Library Cataloguing in Publication Data
Pickford, Tony
    What is it like at the seaside?
    1. Seashore – Juvenile literature 2. Seaside resorts – Juvenile literature
    I. Title
    551.4'57

Acknowledgements
The Publishers would like to thank the following for permission to reproduce photographs:
Bruce Coleman Collection: Gordon Langsbury p24; Collections: Paul Watts pp12, 13, Robin Williams p20, Oliver Benn p26; Ecoscene: John Farmar p22; Environmental Images: Trevor Perry p25, Leslie Garland p27; Eye Ubiquitous: p10, P Craven p4, Tim Page p19, R Battersby p23; Hulton Getty: p9; James Davis Travel Photography: p7; Robert Harding Picture Library: pp6, 15, Jean Brooks p5, Duncan Maxwell p11, R Rainford p14, Rob Cousins p18; Sally and Richard Greenhill: p8; The Photo Library Wales: Steve Peake p21; Tony Pickford: pp16, 17

Cover photograph reproduced with permission of Powerstock Zefa.

Every effort has been made to contact copyright holders of any material reproduced in this book. Any omissions will be rectified in subsequent printings if notice is given to the Publisher.

Contents

Words printed in **bold letters like these** are explained in the Glossary.

What is a seaside?

The seaside is a place where the land meets the sea. It is sometimes called the **coast** or the seashore. Some seaside places have long sandy beaches where you can run and play in the sea. Others have high **cliffs**. You can look down from the cliffs onto sharp rocks.

Hornsea Beach on a busy day with families enjoying the sand and sunshine.

Some towns have grown around places where ships are built. Other seaside towns are places where fishing boats come and go.

Some seaside towns are **ports** where ships bring goods from other countries. Others have become places for people to visit and have holidays. We call these places seaside **resorts**. What is your favourite kind of seaside place?

The crew of this fishing boat is getting ready to go out to sea to catch fish.

A seaside resort

There are many kinds of seaside **resorts**. Some are very quiet and people come to enjoy the beach for a day. Other resorts have places for people to stay, such as guesthouses and hotels.

In big seaside resorts there are funfairs with exciting rides and games to play. There are shops and lots of places to eat and drink.

There are many hotels and guesthouses next to this beach in Llandudno, Wales.

The streets are busy with people in the daytime and at night people come to look at the bright lights along the seashore.

Some resorts were small **villages** in the past. The shops, cafes and hotels were built when people started to come for day trips and holidays. Other seaside resorts were built in places where there were no houses before.

What might you be able to see from the top of the big wheel in this funfair at Blackpool beach?

Now and in the past

What do you like to do when you go to a seaside **resort**? Do you like to visit the funfair and go on the rides? Do you like to go on the beach and build sandcastles? What other things can you do on the beach?

People go to the seaside for day trips or for a holiday. Some people might go to a seaside resort in another country.

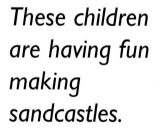

These children are having fun making sandcastles.

In the early 1900s people used to wear their normal clothes to go to the seaside.

In the past, families travelled to the seaside by train or bus. At the seaside they walked along the **pier**.

There were small cabins on the beach for people to change into their swimming costumes. Children paddled in the sea while the grown-ups sat on deckchairs on the beach.

Other kinds of seaside places

Some seaside towns and **villages** are mainly places where people work. Fishing **ports** are special seaside places. Fishing boats catch fish out at sea. There are **quays**, where the boats are tied up. At other ports big ships carry goods to and from other countries.

At this place by the sea there are many caravans and mobile homes where people come to stay.

This empty Scottish beach is a long way from any town or city.

The land can meet the sea in different ways. In some places there are long, empty beaches where the countryside meets the sea.

There might also be long stretches of empty **mudflats** where flocks of birds gather or there can be wet, **marshy** places and sandy hills called dunes.

Tides and seasons

Seaside places can look very different at different times of the day because of the **tide**. Every day the sea moves towards the land and away from it again. This is called the tide.

When the tide is in, the sea rises and covers the beach or the rocks on the seashore. It can be dangerous to play on a beach when the tide is coming in.

The tide is coming in along this rocky shore. It is a dangerous place at this time.

The tide has now gone out along this rocky shore. It is now safe to walk on the sand.

When the tide goes out, the beach and rocks can be seen again. It is good to walk on a beach just after the tide has gone out because it is fresh and clean.

Seaside places can be very different in the summer and in the winter. On sunny summer days, seaside **resorts** are very busy with crowds of people. In winter, when the wind is cold, there are very few people around.

A rocky shore

Some rocky shores have no sand at all. Behind the shore are high **cliffs**. When the **tide** is in, the waves cover the beach and beat against the cliffs.

The sea cuts into the cliffs so that the rocks above hang over and are ready to fall. The pieces of rock that fall off the cliffs are rolled backwards and forwards by the waves until they are worn into smooth, round **pebbles**.

These cliffs by the sea are made of different coloured rocks.

In some places there are tall white cliffs made of a rock called chalk. In other places, the cliffs are made of different rocks so that they are white at the top and red at the bottom.

At rocky seaside places, pools of water are left when the tide goes out. There you can find crabs and other sea creatures.

These children are looking in rock pools to see what the tide has left behind.

A busy port

Glasson Dock is a small **port** on an estuary. An estuary is where a river meets the sea. A **canal** was built a long time ago so that boats could come from nearby towns and cities carrying goods to be loaded onto ships.

A village has grown around the **dock**. There are still boats on the canal, but now they carry people on holiday or day trips. Most goods are now brought to the ports in lorries.

Glasson Dock is on the estuary of the River Lune.

This fertilizer will soon be loaded onto a ship.

When a ship comes into the dock, it is tied up at the **quay**. A **crane** unloads a **cargo** of wood, which is loaded onto lorries to be taken away.

Once the ship is empty, it is loaded with new cargo, this time with white bags of plant food called fertilizer.

A fishing port

This is a busy fishing **port**. Many fishing boats are tied up at the long **quays**. Most fishing boats are painted in bright colours and have small flags that flap in the wind.

The boats are often away for a few days to catch fish. When they go, the port is quiet and empty. The fishermen work, eat and sleep on their boats while they are out at sea. Their boats drag big nets through the water.

These brightly painted fishing boats are ready to go out to sea.

The fishermen's nets are lifted on to the boats and the fish are emptied out. The fish are stored in ice until the boats return to the port.

When the fishing boats return, the fish are taken off in boxes and sold in the buildings on the quayside. Some of the fish will be turned into fish fingers in factories and some will go to local fish and chip shops.

Boxes of fresh fish are sold in the fish market at a fishing port.

Working at the seaside

Some people work in jobs that help people have holidays by the sea. In the big hotels chefs cook food for the people who stay. Every hotel has a receptionist who greets people when they arrive and tells them which room they will be staying in.

Some small boats take people on day trips.

*The harbour-master makes sure all the boats in the **harbour** are safe.*

The lifeboat crew goes out to sea in a small, fast lifeboat if people are in trouble. They might rescue someone who has gone out too far when swimming or help people on a boat in stormy weather.

In seaside resorts, some people collect money for rides on the funfair. Can you think of other jobs that people do at the seaside?

Living by the sea

Do you live by the sea? This is a **village** by the sea. The sea covers the main road to the village twice a day when the **tide** moves in and out. Cars cannot use the road when the sea covers it. People who live in the village have to plan their day so that they do not need to travel when the tide is in.

The tide must go out before it is safe to travel to this village by the sea called Burgh Island.

The cliffs have crumbled away and it is not safe to live in this house anymore.

The cliffs in the picture above are made of soft, crumbly rock. The waves beat against the cliffs and parts of the seashore sometimes crumble into the sea. As the cliffs are worn away, the houses are getting closer to the edge. Strong walls will be built at the foot of the cliffs to protect the houses.

The wild seaside

Some seaside places are far away from big towns and cities. People visit to walk along the seashore or to watch the flocks of seabirds that visit the empty **mudflats** when the **tide** is out.

Next to the beach are sandy hills called dunes. Behind the dunes are wet, **marshy** pools. Other birds make their nests here.

This bird is called an oystercatcher. It feeds on the small creatures that live in the mud.

This area is protected by the Wildfowl and Wetlands Trust.

Do you like visiting wild seaside places? How would you feel if someone wanted to build houses or shops there? Places like this are very special, so there are rules to stop people from building on them. The Royal Society for Protection of Birds and other groups look after many wild seaside places.

Changes at the seaside

Seaside places are changing all the time. New **marinas** or long **quays** have been built. Many small boats are kept there. There are some boats with sails and some fast boats, with noisy engines.

*These new houses have been built at an old **harbour** where ships used to load and unload their **cargoes**.*

This wall helps to protect the seashore from the waves.

Some seaside resorts were very busy places in the past, but have had to change because fewer people come to stay now. Some of the hotels have been changed into flats for people to live in.

In places where the sea is wearing away the seashore, strong walls are built. Sometimes these walls can make the seashore look ugly.

Activities

What do you like to do at the seaside? Make a map or a picture of a seaside place that you would like to visit. Put in all the things that make a seaside place worth visiting. You could draw a **pier** or a funfair. Or perhaps your place will just have a long beach where you can make sandcastles or fly a kite.

How would your favourite seaside place look?

Planning to go on holiday to the seaside can be almost as much fun as being there! People collect holiday **brochures** that show pictures of seaside places in this country and in distant places. Ask an adult to collect some brochures for you to look at. Make your own holiday brochure of seaside places with pictures and writing about holidays by the sea.

Your holiday brochure might look like this.

Find out for yourself

There are many seaside places that you can visit. For example, a big seaside **resort** like Blackpool or a rocky seaside with **cliffs** like Flamborough Head in Yorkshire. You could even visit a fishing **port** like Looe in Cornwall.

Some seaside places are looked after by the Royal Society for the Protection of Birds (RSPB). You can join the RSPB children's club, Wildlife Explorers. To find out more, go to – www.rspb.org.uk

The Wildfowl and Wetlands Trust protects places where geese, ducks and seabirds visit the seashore. Visit the Trust's website – www.wwt.org.uk

To find out about the important work done by lifeboats, visit www.rnli.org.uk

Glossary

brochure a booklet that shows pictures of holiday resorts

canal a kind of river built by people

cargo the things carried by a ship

cliff steep rocky land next to the sea

coast the edge of the land next to the sea

crane a big machine for lifting things

dock a place where ships are loaded, unloaded, built or mended

harbour a place where boats can safely stay when they are not at sea

marina a place where many small boats stay when they are not at sea

marsh a piece of very wet ground

mudflat very flat sand and mud which can only be seen when the tide is out

pebble a small stone that has been made smooth by the sea

pier a long platform that is built over the sea for people to walk on

port a place where ships load and unload the things that they carry

quay part of a port or harbour where ships and boats are tied up

resort a place where people go for visits or holidays

tide the movement of the sea toward the land and away from the land

village a group of houses and other buildings in the country

Index